BROKEN CRUSTS

BROKEN CRUSTS

SONGS OF FAITH AND FREEDOM

Selected Poems by

Clifford J. Laube

Arx Publishing
Merchantville, NJ

Arx Publishing,
Merchantville, NJ

Broken Crusts: Songs of Faith and Freedom
Selected Poems by Clifford J. Laube

Grateful acknowledgment is made to *The New York Times*,
*The Sign, Spirit, The Commonweal, Queen of All Hearts,
The Monasticon* and *The Aeonian*, in which certain of these
poems first appeared.

First Edition

ISBN 978-1-889758-73-2

Library of Congress Cataloging-in-Publication Data

Laube, Clifford J.
  Broken crusts : songs of faith and freedom : selected
poems / by Clifford J. Laube. -- 1st ed.
    p. cm.
  ISBN 978-1-889758-73-2
  I. Title

PS3523.A784B76 2007
811'.52--dc22

                                        2007020716

CONTENTS

CONTENTS (continued)

CONTENTS (continued)

ABOUT THE AUTHOR

Clifford J. Laube was born on August 28, 1891 in Telluride, southwest Colorado, to Adolph and Alma (James) Laube, a prospecting couple. His father was a lapsed Catholic and his mother a Congregationalist. Despite the poverty and hardships of his early years, the awe-inspiring natural beauty of his Colorado surroundings made a lifelong impression on him, expressed vividly in much of his poetry. Due to the breakdown of his mother's health when he was six years old, his father was forced to place him and his three siblings in St. Vincent's orphanage in Denver for six years. It was here, under the loving care of the Daughters of Charity, that Laube "breathed the atmosphere of Catholic life at its purest and best," as he would say years later. At the age of twelve, with his father's permission, he was baptized into the Catholic Church. This gift of the Faith would become the driving force of his entire life. When his father died years later, he too had become an ardent, practicing Catholic again.

Laube's journalistic career began when his father opened a newspaper in Rico, their hometown. He wished to further his education and saw little prospect of it in the rustic mining town of Rico, so against his father's wishes he left home and completed his high school studies in Durango (he was Valedictorian of his graduating class). He then returned home, was reconciled with his father, and took over editorship of the paper, The Rico Item. In 1916, he was elected to the Colorado State Legislature. Afterwards, he worked as a reporter for the Denver Times for three years.

During an excursion East with his young wife, Dora, to visit her family in Ohio, the couple decided to see New York. A chance meeting on the streets of the Big City with his boss's son, who worked for The New York Daily News, landed him a job as a reporter for that paper. This visit and its consequences are the subject of his poem, *Towers*. In three years he had moved on from a reporter to Assistant City Editor. After eight years with the paper, he received a position on the staff of The New York Times as Suburban Editor and remained with the paper for over twenty-four years, retiring as Day National News Editor in 1953.

Laube was chairman of the executive board of the Catholic Poetry Society of America from 1934 to 1937 and was co-founder of its magazine, *Spirit*. He was president of the Society from 1955 to 1961. In 1947, he was elected to the Gallery of Living Catholic Authors in recognition of his service to Catholic letters.

In 1937, he established in the cellar of his home in Ozone Park, New York, the Monastine Press, named after his favorite saints, St. Monica and St. Augustine. From his basement workshop Laube produced a number of volumes of poetry among which were his own volume, *Crags*, as well as *The Sword* by Helene Searcy Puls, *The Last Garland* by Theodore Maynard, *Journey with Music* by Frances Maguire, *Wings Over Patmos* by Charles A. Brady, *Rind and All* by Joseph Tusiani, and Jessica Powers's first book of poetry, *The Lantern Burns*.

He was also poetry editor of the Passionist Fathers' magazine, *The Sign*, and *Queen of All Hearts* magazine, published by the Montfort Fathers, until his death in 1974.

Despite the fact that his formal education went no further than high school, Laube's activities in the field of literature, journalism and education earned him four honorary doctorates from Fordham University, Boston College, St. Bonaventure College, and Manhattan College.

But over and above his career accomplishments, his most outstanding characteristic was his deep and ardent Catholic Faith. He had an almost mystical love of God's unstained creation. The whole created order was magical to him—full of God's own 'magic'. Yet, he also had no less admiration for the creative work of man who participates, through his God-given talents, in the work of the Creator. He not only never disdained technology, provided it was ordered to good, but he marveled at it with the same awe with which he beheld a sunset. To him, both were reflections of God's creative love, and especially man, who is the apex of God's creation and whose cooperation with his Creator magnifies and glorifies Him.

For those of us who knew and loved Clifford Laube, his poem of poems, *Renewal* (page 117), expresses his heart and soul through and through. The grace of his childhood faith, "When I was twelve years old I vowed," filled the whole horizon of his life until on August 21st, 1974, one week before his 83rd birthday, he surrendered it consciously and peacefully to the Lord he had loved and served so faithfully.

And so that light I swear to keep
Till I have stumbled down the steep
To my last hope-illumined sleep.

ART CREDITS

The woodcuts appearing on pages 46 and 68 were done by **Clifford J. Laube** himself and originally appeared in *Crags*.

The illustrations on pages 30 and 78 were made by **Anne Marie Sohler,** a great-granddaughter of Clifford Laube who is currently a junior at Franciscan University of Steubenville.

The illustration on page 40 was created by **Jaclyn A. Warren**, fiancée of **Daniel Tully**, a great-grandson of Clifford Laube.

The illustrations on pages 4, 17, and 118 were created by **Sister Magdalene, OCD,** a granddaughter of Clifford Laube and a contemplative nun at Philadelphia Carmel. She also developed the cover design concept and the rose-breaks that appear throughout the book. Sr. Magdalene has a degree in illustration and design from Tyler School of Art.

Katharine Sohler, a great-granddaughter of Clifford Laube, assisted with data entry, design, page composition, and other aspects of production.

The photo of Clifford Laube on the book's back cover was taken by **Kathy Daley**, his eldest granddaughter.

The photo on the upper back cover of the Falls of San Miguel, Telluride, Colorado, was taken by **Esther Laube**, wife of **Cliff Laube**, the author's son, during their excursion west in 1998.

*"Piercingly at the crisis of the Mass
(White heartbreak of the Host!)..."*
(**Particles**, page 6)

PROLOGUE

PARTICLES

So what is beauty but a tremble of bloom
On fragile things uplifted to the light?
Forever since the ether pools were stirred
And scattered into bubbles of new worlds,
Forever since the million-bladed grass
Broke the first clod, behold that living gleam!

O delicate and prodigal delight!
I saw it early. It still dazzles me.

I saw it early on the splintered crags;
I marked its lustre in the broken quartz.
I saw it in renewals of the rain
And in swift waters under running cloud.
Through many tumults of entangled leaves
It moved, and in the mossy silences.
By fabulous steel terraces and towers
I see it now and still it dazzles me.

Whose hand and purpose stirred the ether pools?
Who shattered light into a toss of stars?

Piercingly at the crisis of the Mass
(White heartbreak of the Host!) an answer came;
"You cannot bear more beauty than I bring
In flakes and fragments for your daily bread.
According to your need, with broken crusts,
My son, I feed you from the infinite."

"We are the sad inheritors of haste,
Sons of distraction, fevered from the start."
(**Cry Out of Babylon**, page 10)

CRY OUT OF BABYLON

CRY OUT OF BABYLON

We are the sad inheritors of haste,
　　Sons of distraction, fevered from the start.
With desolation is our hope made waste
　　Because no man has quiet in his heart.

Yet through the din of these disordered years
　　Truth's Bride, still unenslaved and unenticed
Utters her old entreaty, touched with tears:
　　"Put first things first. Think with the mind of Christ."

Think with the mind of Christ? The rule is hard;
　　Yes, doubly hard amid this hellish grind
Of wheels and words. But oh, the rich reward:
　　To be a cell in the supernal Mind!

PRAYER OUT OF IMPERFECTION

Lord, drawn to Thee by that dread lifted up
    Which Thou didst say must draw all men to Thee,
My wedding garment soiled, I dare to sup
    The chaliced essence of Thy charity.

With proudflesh still an ache upon my heart
    I come, a child of pardon, to repay
What love I can, till that which is in part
    And still imperfect shall be done away.

PRAYER FOR PERSEVERANCE

How many times, how many years
    This heart has cried its filial claim
To innocence untouched of tears
    And love beyond the reach of blame.

Still unappeased, the panting breast
    Can only crave a little sleep.
Eve's ancient fever will not rest,
    And Adam's malady is deep.

O Breath from Love's abyss! O balm!
    O Christ Who conquered hell's intrigue,
Sustain me. You have heard my psalm;
    You know the famine, the fatigue.

Prayer Against Reprobation

In that fixed penal day of last decrees
    When hope and fear alike shall stand afraid,
And only innocence shall be at ease,
    Seeing the host of witnesses arrayed,

Faith, fail me not, lest I be stricken dumb
    With dismal shame at my demerit mark.
Let one last murmured *mea culpa* come
    Between my desperation and the dark.

Haply a listener along that rim
    Of strict arraignment, hearing my poor plea,
Will testify: "Once thou didst walk with Him
    Who judgest here. Thy speech betrayeth thee."

SUFFICIENT GRACE

He who prays and has prayed
    For a love without lust,
For a heart unafraid
    And a star he can trust
When the figureheads fade
    In the darkness of dust,

In so far as his prayer
    Couples purpose to thought
When his will takes the dare,
    He will have what he sought,
Light and strength, and to spare,
    Though he reckon it not.

Signum et Crux

Faced by a never resting Foe,
    What fears and what defeats were mine
Did not this heavenly Auspice glow
    For me as once for Constantine!

Yet I am humbled, having scored
    A triumph or retrieved a loss,
Knowing that this my standard, Lord,
    Is but the sign. You had the Cross.

REEDS

Whether soft airs stir lightly
    Or angered winds be harsh,
The living reeds lean sprightly
    Along the marsh.

Who has not seen them lifting
    Their shining assegais
Under the free and drifting
    Foam of the skies?

Once for a King impassioned
    With truth, yet sore betrayed,
There was a scepter fashioned
    From such a blade.

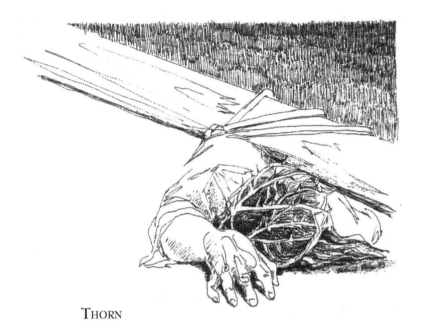

THORN

Wherever the brown soil is sunned
    And watered, and bright tendrils rise,
One stem has stood despised and shunned
    Since Adam lost his paradise.

This is the thorn that lay in wait
    (Ah, woe of wept Jerusalem!)
Ready for maliced hands to plait
    Into a mocking diadem.

Redemptive root! It pierced Him sore
    And thus became a sacred thing:
The only crown He ever wore
    Who was in truth a King.

Lord, Thy Delight

Fresh from Thine altar in the morning air,
Faith takes sweet meditation as its share
Of savor from the Eucharistic fare.

Thus to the lifted mind there comes again
Thy Wisdom-word: "To be with sons of men
Is my delight." O word beyond our ken!

Canst Thou have joy in us of tainted seed,
Whose hearts are hunger and whose love is need,
With Adam-glory marred and atrophied?

Rather it is our gladness to break bread
With Thee, and thus refreshed and healed and fed,
To hear Thy gentle "Sursum corda" said.

But oh, the counterpart: We cannot quite,
Even with Host-fed strength, essay its height:
That *Thou, Who hast no longing, hast delight!*

"Mystical star above the slope,
Mother of men, be thou our hope!"
(**Ave, Vita Nostra!**, page 22)

AVE, VITA NOSTRA!

AVE, VITA NOSTRA!

Attila's spirit rides again the red roads of the East;
    Caligula returns, a subtler tyrant, to the South;
King Herod's sword still seeks the Lord; with fury thrice increased
    It strikes at holy youth and maims the manna-nourished mouth.

    Mother of God, amid this strife,
    Amid this death, be thou our life!

Dark intellects like Lucifer's, low-fallen in their pride,
    Have dimmed the philosophic lamp in Learning's ancient seats;
Despoiled of grace, a godless race thrusts purity aside,
    Slaying the lily in its bulb, the heart before it beats.

    Mother of Christ's integrity,
    Amid this blight, our sweetness be.

Yet while the Coliseums stand, the catacombs remain.
    The wolf pack prowls, but Peter watches, faithful to his flock.
A martyred Pro in Mexico, the mangled priests of Spain,
    The hidden saints of Russia, show the texture of the Rock.

    Mystical star above the slope,
    Mother of men, be thou our hope!

Hail, holy Queen!
Mother of mercy,
Our *life*, our *sweetness* and our *hope*,
To thee do we cry, poor banished children of Eve.
To thee do we send up our sighs,
Mourning and weeping in this valley of tears.

TRUCE

Still strives the spirit to control
    Material tissue. Still is sued
The body's siege against the soul.
    Ah, the sad and immemorial feud!

But once they met in a white truce
    Beneath the more than maiden breast
Of one whom sin dared not seduce,
    Et Verbum caro factum est.

Spirit and fiber in one mesh
    Immaculate were fused and sealed.
The Word has sanctified the flesh.
    Let the old enmity be healed.

CANTICLE ON THE MOTHER OF CHRIST

Forever since she sang
Her ancillary song:
"Let it be done to me
According to Thy word;"
Forever since she sang
Her visitation song:
"My spirit has rejoiced
In God my Saviour,"
Her own have shared her chant
And, singing to her,
Clinging to her,
Calling her Gabriel-wise
"Most full of grace
 And blessed among woman,"
Have made her prophecy
A living fact fulfilled.

England indeed had hope
When it was Mary's land,
Naming the meadows-flowers
And all the wayside shrines
For her in honor bright.
Italy, Poland, France
Under her queenly sway
Raised up their noblest spires,
Spilling a jewel-light
Upon the altared Mass,

Making all art celestial
For her sake and her Son's.

No sea-wind's wild caprice
Could stay the Marian sails
By which Columbus came
To hope's new continent.
So too will Peter's barque
Under her guiding star
Come safely into port.

Dark Lucifer has known
The crushing of her heel.
Thus did the infidel
In fierce Lepanto's clash
Cower to feel her sting.

Ask now the Baltic serfs,
Ask all the scattered saints
Of Ukraine and the steppes;
Ask overrun Cathay
How many regiments
Christ's earthly Vicar has.
Strong will the answer come:
As many as the hosts
Of Mary's legionnaires.

Only the virgin wax,
Only the lily and rose

Dare glow at Mary's feet.
Only beloved John
Whose bosom chaste had felt
The heartbeat of her Son,
Was worthy to receive
After cold Calvary
The leaning of her breast.

Now all the desolate
Will find their sorrow sweet
When tinctured with her love,
Her pity and her tears.

ESTHER'S DARING

O more than beauty, more than noble bearing
    Met peril in that court of last appeal
Where startled eunuchs paled at Esther's daring,
    Their scimitars upraised to daunt her zeal.
Bold and unbidden, steeled in her reliance
    Upon the God of Hosts, she ventured there,
Pitting against the price for such defiance
    Her protocol of pity and of prayer.

      Ahasuerus held his breath
      To see such icy scorn of death,
      Then dipped his scepter, proud to give
      True valor its prerogative.
      And so she stood there free, elate,
      Her people's fiery advocate.

Prefigured thus on Truth's eternal pages,
    We see what centuries of saints have seen:
Before a higher King, desired of ages,
    Arrayed in whiter robes, another Queen.
Perfect in grace, all-powerful in pleading,
    Chaste Virgin-Mother of Immanuel,
Royal, she offers for our interceding
    Christ's conquest over all the courts of hell.

      Unchallenged is her right to bring
      Our supplications to the King.
      Through her, redemption's chosen door,
      Christ's merits and his mercies pour;
      And never Haman but shall feel
      The bruise, the crushing of her heel.

EARLIER WITNESS

Count it not strange that Mary, of all creatures
    Elect and beautiful, untouched of blight,
Was not to see her Son's transfigured features
    With Peter, James and John on Thabor's height.

Her breast had been His halo. Through long morrows
    Of mothering she watched him; through the toss
Of multitudes and tempters; through the sorrows
    That brought Him to the thorn-crown and the Cross.

She wept and bled with Him at every station
    Of Calvary, yet rightly Holy Writ
Records her not at His transfiguration:
    She *knew* His glory. She was part of it.

THE PERFECT PART

> Mary has chosen the best part, and it will not be
> taken from her. —St. Luke 10:42

This was the perfect part, the calling sweet
    Which Mary chose:
To sit in silence at the Saviour's feet
    As a white rose
With petals open to the Paraclete.

That trust, that tenderness, that drawing near
    As listener
And intercessor, intimate and dear,
    Remains with her.
So runs the Scripture, and the word is clear.

Still suppliant before the Living Host,
    She offers thus
The perfume of her pleading where it most
    Avails for us
With God the Father, Son and Holy Ghost.

"Yet innocence, by heaven's grace..."
(**Magdalen,** page 33)

ANCHORED IN TRUTH

To Saint Augustine

Your halo, spun from Monica's pure tears
    Fused with white gold of intellectual grace,
Startles me not. Across the twilight years
    I take your hand and seem to know your face.

For I have tasted the strong heresies
    And felt the stirrings of illusioned flesh,
Only to find the sting you found in these
    And turn to Living Waters cool and fresh.

With you I seem to walk the crowded ways
    Of Carthage, and in Hippo's dusty streets
Laurel your eloquence with my poor praise,
    Glad of your triumphs, grieved at your defeats.

O vehement heart, tell me of that fond one
    Whose pagan charm was your pathetic snare.
And what of him, the little lad, your son
    Adeodatus? Had he golden hair?

Echoes my spirit with your plaintive cry:
    "Too late, too late have I discovered Thee,
Thou Ancient beauty!" But the saints espy,
    Anchored in Truth, your immortality.

Prayer to the Beloved Disciple

Thou who wert singled for His last bequest
   On that Cross-anchoring crest:
The care of her whose fruited chastity,
   Fulfilled upon the Tree,
Was free from stain, yet not from sorrow free;

Thou who the night before (O holiest test!)
   For very sympathy
Didst dare to lean upon the Saviour's breast
   In eucharistic rest,
At my last supper let me lean on thee.

Magdalen

No art, no ray can reillume
A wilted waterlily's bloom;

Nor any alchemy reclaim
A once-extinguished flame.

Yet innocence, by heaven's grace,
Shone again in Mary's face.

THE SNATCH OF ST. STEPHEN

You had a right to slay him, Saul;
    To curse with those who cried him down,
To hold their coats and watch him fall
    And hear his words of pardon drown
    In martyrdom outside the town.

Your deed was well within the law,
    But Stephen's was a braver code.
That holy face whose Light you saw
    Accused you as it later glowed
    Undimmed on the Damascus road.

It was that look he lanced at you,
    The fierce forgiveness as he fell,
With Christ's compassion piercing through,
    That made your proud epistles tell
    How pity plucked you out of hell.

TO SAUL OF TARSUS

Until that day when Mercy caught you riding
    With angry spur down the Damascus road,
What foe had merited immortal chiding
    From Him whose heart with red redemption flowed?

No clemency through Pilate's dark proceeding
    Sought He who silent faced the rabble's wrath;
Plaintive to you alone His voice came pleading
    That murmured never once on Calvary's path.

For you those singular sad accents calling:
    "Saul, Saul, why hast thou persecuted me?"
Were the last petals of His Passion falling,
    Late tokens of remembered agony.

But oh, the bittersweet in their complaining
    Was balm to you in afterdays forlorn,
For then your heart, though barbed by bitter paining,
    Once having breathed the Rose, could bear the thorn.

To Gamaliel

Gamaliel, prophetic Pharisee,
    Because you feared the Lord and loved the Law,
I think you found a blest eternity
    Steeped in the holy Light that Stephen saw.

A record stained in apostolic tears
    Bears witness how, before a sullen mob,
You shielded Christ's commissioned pioneers
    With words that still restrain, still nobly throb.

"Let these men be!" Your stringent accents stung;
    "If this work be of men it needs must fail;
But if it be of God no fury flung
    Against its sure foundation shall prevail."

And then the solemn sequel, meetly crowned
    With motive supernatural, unflawed
By human sanction: "Heed lest ye be found
    To fight against the hidden hand of God!"

Thus you who, fearing God, feared not the wrath
    Of men, rebuked their blind unrighteous ire
And sped once more upon the Gospel path
    Those heroes tongued with Paracletian fire.

Time proves your test. What those Apostles built
 Has stood through centuries of stress and shock:
Behold, where apostolic blood was spilt,
 Rises immune the bold Tiberian Rock!

Rabbi, the Old Law and the New are one
 In this evangel: There is mercy stored
Where secrets of the living truth are spun
 For those who love the Law and fear the Lord.

Therefore it is my faith, brave Pharisee,
 That in your soul baptismal graces gleamed,
And that you now stand justified and free
 In the assembly of the glad redeemed.

To Thomas the Apostle

Not yours the cynic sneer
　　But a redeemable doubt—
A plaintive, sad, sincere
　　Passion for finding out;
So for your sake He came
　　Past bolted doors to chide
With sanctifying shame,
　　And let your fingers hide
　　Within His wounded side.

ENCYCLICAL

"Simon," the Master said, "I bid thee keep
    Thy vessel farther from these shallow frets
Of surf and shore. Launch out into the deep,
    And there let down thy nets."

Obedient the Fisherman updrew
    The weedy drags. His boat with even glide
Found deeper waters where the doubting crew
    Once more the tackle plied.

The nets closed in. Straightway the boat was brimmed
    And gleaming with a scaly silver hoard.
Simon, astonished, gasped. With eyes bedimmed,
    He trembled to his Lord.

Ages of surf on shore! And now again
    The Fisherman is signaled from the shoals;
His new Genesareth a sea of men,
    His prize immortal souls.

The Barque of Christ strains for the catch. It sets
    From its safe mooring. Tide is at the neap.
Peter, with strange unseen Marconian nets,
    Launches into the deep.

"Winged as a white dove, Gently the Spirit came..."
(**Three Things**, page 45)

THE PETALED FIRE

THE PETALED FIRE

None had a tenderer prayer
Or holier right to pray
Than they,
The chosen Twelve, close-gathered there
In intimate last sharing of His board,
Who whispered, "Lord,
Leave us not desolate, but stay!"

Yet He,
The ever loving and the gentle-willed
Who once had stilled
The tempest-tumult over Galilee,
Now firmly facing His own agony
Could brave a bitter *"No;*
It is expedient that I should go."

Not then, not then
In that most bleak denial and farewell,
Could those poor men
With pained surmisal and imperfect ken
Perceive the greater good;
But later, when the petaled fire fell
Within the cenacle, they understood.

So when in gloom,
Sad supplicant, my soul, your prospects darken,
Yielding no word
Or sign responsive to your tears' demand,
Retire awhile and hearken
In holy resignation's upper room.
There silence will be stirred
By Pentecostal breath and fiery bloom;
There will the Paraclete be heard,
And you will understand.

THE QUICKENER

Who by intimation knows
Where the Holy Spirit blows?
What inertia can resist
That inpowering pull and twist?

Never hand shall hold or hire
Forces of that agile Fire
Seldom caught, too lightly lost,
Pride-eluding Pentecost!

Yet, as evil strikes to kill
Where it finds a furtive will,
So God's whistling Breath will stir
Toward the leaning listener.

Did not saintly Simeon,
Patient for the Promised One,
Hear in vigils, prayer-engrossed,
Pantings of the Holy Ghost?

Pharisaic hands and feet
Could not snare the Paraclete;
Thirteen in an Upper Room
Felt and saw the Fiery Plume.

THREE THINGS

Winged as a white dove,
    Gently the Spirit came
To brush with brooding love
    That brow which bore our blame.

Flame-petaled Pentecost
    Shone in a secret room
Where Thirteen prayed, and tossed
    On each a fiery plume.

There spoke the palpable Power
    In syllables of wind,
Sealing in one swift hour
    What time shall not rescind.

Ever the heart must stir
    At thought of these three things:
Fire and wind and the whir
    Of white mysterious wings.

"Lizard Head, star-thirsty stone..."
(**To Lizard Head**, page 48)

THE CRAGS OF HOME

To Lizard Head

Lizard Head, star-thirsty stone,
 Fang at the face of the sky,
Fierce as you are and alone,
 You are not more so than I.

There is a peer to your pride
 Under the starry patrol.
Haughtier silences ride
 Past the sharp crest of my soul.

Flaunt your ephemeral fires
 Where the stray meteors spill!
Light from no star that expires
 Suns the white shaft of my will.

Arrogant rock, one bold hour
 Out of time's reach I shall thrust;
Something within me will tower
 When you are talus and dust.

SOLITUDE

The shadow of a crag was on my birth
    And on my youth the shadow of a pine.
High on a bleak shelf of the faulted earth
    Long mysteries of solitude were mine.
Old Mount Dolores in her icy shawl
    Was my strict foster-mother. From her frost
The cold doom of a desolate waterfall
    Poured thunder down the Valley of the Lost.
There voices babbled not, but every sound
    Was sharp and certain. On the lonely steep
Tall men—not of the multitude—I found
    With strong grave faces worth a memory's keep.
By these austerities that I have known,
If need be I can dare to stand alone.

THE FALLS OF SAN MIGUEL

Where cold crag-shadows fall
    Across the trestled flumes
    And trams of Telluride,
Flash three perpetual
    Suspended water-plumes,
      Three banners that abide.
        Cornet and Bridal Veil
          Over ledge and steep;
          Sheer by the Tomboy trail
          Ingram's wild leap!

The loosed snow-thunder's roar,
    Swift as a bolt of thought,
      Strikes grandly and is done.
But these doomed waters pour
    Perilous, ceasing not
      Under the stars and sun.
        Foam-spray and diamond-hail,
          Harps on the steep;
          Cornet and Bridal Veil,
          Ingram's wild leap!

THE DARK PINE

This fibered beauty, this cool bark,
This harmony of height and girth,
These wafted plumes at heaven's arc
Are things of earth, yet not of earth.

There is a Breath upon my brow,
And in my soul a certain Sign,
Else I would kneel, a Druid, now,
Idolatrous of this dark pine.

I swear this is no mortal tree;
No perishable root would dare
To stand in such sublimity,
Exhaling a celestial air.

Who drew my dreaming to this hill?
Who set this snare? A falling cone
Alone responds. Some hidden will
Is overshadowing my own.

My feet are lost. I am waylaid.
There is a witness watching me:
Beauty from her bright balconade
Leans like a living deity.

O Being, thus superbly seen,
Betray me not upon the steep.
O god of this dark evergreen,
Beware! I have my soul to keep.

SHARERS OF THE SUN

Legion the meadow daisies mass
Where pageants of the summer pass.

More shy, the sego lilies hide
Singly upon the mountain-side.

Those sky-clad elfins of the snow,
Blue columbines, in clusters blow.

Thus sistered, sole or scattered far,
Star differeth from sepaled star;

Yet each is fair, and every one
Gladly receives its share of sun.

CHLOROPHYL

For whose expected feet
Are the invisible looms
On valley-floor and hill
    Forever weaving,
Weaving the moss, the sweet
Rich grass in emerald glooms,
    The velvet chlorophyl?

Go to the wilderness
And follow a swift stream.
Forget its music. Mark
    How it goes weaving,
Weaving cool water-cress
Where ferns and willows dream
Through daylight and the dark.

Never a forest pool,
Never sequestered spring
But teems with living hosts:
    Green algae, weaving,
Weaving without a spool
Soft sumptuous carpeting
Meet for the tread of ghosts.

WILD STRAWBERRY BLOSSOMS

O central Light, if there had been no cluster
    Of Pleiades, nor any nightly star,
I would have known Thee by the gentler luster
    That gleams where wild strawberry blossoms are.

There was a path on Piedmont's sunny shoulder;
    It rambled idly through an aspen grove;
And there by minted bank and mossy boulder
    Those early blooms were my first treasure-trove.

Was it not joy enough just to be breathing
    Sweet May on equal terms with fern and tree?
Yet here were hints of petaled heaven wreathing
    About my feet a floral galaxy.

White wonder touched me. I was overtaken.
    That hour a revelation came to pass;
For thus the light heart of a lad was shaken
    To find a glory scattered in the grass.

REGATTA IN CLOUD

I flung myself upon a mossy hill
    And watched the clouds like royal navies race
For my delight. There, with an eager will,
    Slaking my spirit at the springs of space,
I drank exhilaration to my fill.

From the cool upland rose a wide expanse
    Of whitecapped sky. The slope was mine alone.
Never a sound came near except perchance
    Some syllable of wing or windy tone
Amid low leaves. All heaven was in my glance.

Mobile the many-sailed flotillas sped
    Across the cobalt skyscape. Caravels
Came on in pomp with stately canvas-spread;
    Next brigantines along the billowy swells,
Then frigates framed in spume and vaporhead.

So passed the skyey squadrons, and for days
    My azured mind was full of flying cloud;
And still my thoughts, like sails once kissed by sprays,
    Blow back to that bright hill where I was proud
To hold the fleets of heaven in my gaze.

To a Water Ousel

Never by channels of quiet
   Blurs the grey whisk of your wing,
      Flash in the form of a bird!
Only where waters at riot
   Swirl in swift torrents that spring
      Snow-born, your piping is heard.

River-enchantment is on you,
   Keeping your heartbeats in bond;
      Harps of the spray hold you thrall;
Else what wild spirit has drawn you
   Here to these heights and beyond
      Where the cold cataracts call?

Never a road but the river
   Offers a lure to your flight;
      Vainly the world calls away;
Willows aslant and aquiver
   Lattice your track of delight;
      Pebbles lie cool for your play.

Rapt, I have watched you at revel
   Many a reverie long
      Chasing your shade in the stream,
Racing the riffles in level
   Arrowy flight, and your song
      Gripping my soul like a dream.

SPRAY

Who watches at the window-sills
    Of wonder, scanning heaven's face,
Drinks of an essence that distills
    Through din and silence out of space.

Ever with intermittent spray
    Of stars and petals and cool rain,
Dewing the eaves of night and day,
    A fragrance drifts to our domain.

Even the cold impassive snow
    Sifts down a crystal heraldry,
And in the frost bright signets glow
    For any simple eye to see.

So rides an energy along
    The universal thoroughfares,
While dusts of dream and spores of song
    Impollen all the wandering airs.

Ever the aromatic breath
    Of God is blowing by. It fills
The aisles of life, the sails of death,
    The rustling garments of the hills.

ECHO TO A COLORADO LYRIC

A tang of altitude is on these lines;
 They lift like aspens in an Ophir grove;
The words are cool as sky-cool columbines
 Where only Colorado winds may rove.

These lines are breath to me. I know the moods
 That mothered all their frosty metaphors;
The piercing Silverton star-solitudes,
 The lure of trails, the hint of hidden ores.

Here Rico is recaptured in a phrase;
 Here old Ouray repeats her canyon-call
To one who loved wild airs on upland ways,
 Gulches and crags...ferns by a waterfall.

BLEAK PARTING

Bitter with dark denial was that day
   Whose sharp recall is still a bitter wine;
I could not speak the words I strove to say,
   For granite was your will and granite mine.

There was no godspeed in your glance for me.
   I turned in the cold mist to the cold train;
And as the coaches started I could see
   The crags of home receding in the rain.

"They say a curse of steel is on this isle
Where rivets swarm amid encrusted stone..."
(**Mid-City Midnight,** page 67)

SIGHTED TOWERS

TOWERS

I tell you this: beware of distant towers.
　　There is a fatal light on castled stone;
And he whose sight that glamour overpowers
　　Thenafter lives a dream, but not his own.
Once I was happy on a western hill
　　And free as the swift waters at its base;
Wild mountain laurel touched my window-sill
　　And mossy paths were all about the place.
But I beheld dim spires in the East,
　　Remote as legendary Ilium;
A fever shook me and it has not ceased;
　　The turrets called. I could not choose but come.
Still in my heart the Western headlands burn,
But I am spellbound. I shall not return.

Clifford J. Laube

AT THE BATTERY SEA-WALL

From inland ledges I had dreamed this bay,
    Guessing its glamour with a boy's surmise;
Now at the sea-wall, leaning toward the spray,
    I store the living harbor in my eyes.

Is this the brine that broke in amber foam
    Against the cleave of Verrazano's prow?
Are these the roads the Half Moon dared to roam?
    Where are the Nyacks and their kinsmen now?

Behind me rises tiered, colossal steel,
    Terraced, and plumed with bannerets of steam;
Before me ferries glide and lighters reel
    And tugs go throbbing by, and sirens scream.

An old tramp freighter slinks in, weather-stained,
    Scaring the sea gulls with an angry snort.
O sight more fabulous than I had feigned!
    I am a stranger in an alien port.

MANHATTAN TURRETS

Ah, surely they were Gothic fires
That forged this steel and edged these spires;
Else how, with such a daring thrust,
Could they dream upward from the dust?

Yet of these turrets not one tells
The tidings of those glad old bells
That once made Gothic arch and truss
Momentous with the *Angelus!*

See how cathedral lights and shades
Prism these windowed palisades!
This towered town will yet breed men
To wake the Gothic soul again.

Lone Ailanthus

One lone ailanthus tree
   By these barbaric walls
Keeps a brave reverie
   Unbroken. Darkness falls.

Here is a dream's last stand
   In traffic's fierce deploy:
One boon the builder's hand,
   Brushing, dared not destroy.

Here Steel, the god of stress,
   Rearing his turrets high,
Concedes to loveliness
   One remnant of the sky.

Night, from hid jewel-swarms,
   Has still three stars to spare
For these uplifted arms
   In this unsylvan air.

Piped Water

Caught in these iron veins are countless rills
That once were mirth and music in the hills.
Here, docile to the valve, impeded flows
The cool and crystal serum of the snows.

These labyrinthine waters once could toss
In sparkling sunlight over mountain moss.
Once they could throw a pearl and satin plume
Across the spillway of a miner's flume.

By busy timber camp and sawmill sluice
They knew the birch's shadow and the spruce.
They heard their own soft thunder and the call
Of ousels winging toward the waterfall.

Here the quick essence of the cloud and wave,
Ensnared and shackled, has become a slave.
Utility is king. His founts contain
The tears but not the laughter of the rain.

MID-CITY MIDNIGHT

They say a curse of steel is on this isle
　　Where rivets swarm amid encrusted stone,
Yet gazing here at midnight's dark profile
Across ten thousand thrusts of starlit tile,
　　I think of grandeur on a Gothic throne.

Beyond this bastion, a beacon's grope
　　In the immense basilica of night
Pierces like prayer, the burnished spear of hope;
And there are ancient signs on heaven's slope
　　For men to read in masonry's despite.

I say these summits, like the Matterhorn,
　　Hide in their crevices the roots of bloom.
God in the ghetto will not be forsworn,
And Sharon's gentle Rose dared to be born
　　In a dark city where there was no room.

"There was a path on Piedmont's sunny shoulder..."
(**Wild Strawberry Blossoms**, page 54)

SPENT HOLIDAY

SPENT HOLIDAY

The furlough's over. The bright interval
    Of rest and freedom fades. Those glancing hours
In whose leaf-filtered light no dream was dull
    Are vanished like the dust-gold of sunflowers.

Once more the brown road meets the busy track
    Of commerce, and insistent signals call
To stern desk-discipline. No turning back
    For a last glimpse of the cool waterfall!

But in the mind there is a rich reserve
    Of images too lovely to forget:
The bridge, the barn, the swallow's airy swerve,
    The rain-washed willow's graceful minuet.

Remembered idyls by a mossy log
    Remain, and when the first-frost cricket shrills,
Fancy will hear at dusk the farmer's dog
    Barking across the hollows of the hills.

PEGGY'S COVE

An alien, driven by an alien sail,
    I came by some bright magic to your town,
And there at the blue cove you gave me hail,
Letitia, limpid-eyed and lotus-pale,
    Wearing Acadian beauty like a crown.

How had I won my way to this delight?
    Voices of children in a blueberry patch;
Wild orchids, rocks, a legendary sight
Of thundering surf, and at the hint of night
    Your hand, the lifting of a friendly latch.

By these a dream came back that I had lost
    Somewhere along the clay-encrusted years.
Now let the sun go down and let the frost
Take all my garlands. Careless of their cost,
    I shall be tranquil when the long night nears.

For in my mind there is a marble grace
    Forever caught, although its hour was brief
As when before Pygmalion's tranced face
Pale Galatea in a starlit space
    Shone bridelike, beautiful beyond belief.

To an Old Fence

Familiar fence, your rugged grace
Knits friendliness about this place.
You brace your sturdy arms around
The homestead with its patch of ground,
Then zigzag in a careless way
Where vines and berry bushes stray.
A glow of sunlit dreaming blurs
Along your gentle barriers.

A boy, I watched the day burn down
From silver rails beyond the town,
And often from cool pasture-bars
Tarried with twilight and with stars.
There in the hush my heart caught hints
Of truth that have not tarnished since.
Remembering that debt, I bless
Your straggling, wayside restfulness.

CRABAPPLE TREE

The place ran wild. I came there without quest,
    A pensive rambler down an idle road;
But what I found was fire in the breast,—
    Ambers of autumn over fields unmowed.

The farmhouse leaned, a derelict abode,
    The shell of some old dream long dispossessed,
But out beyond the barn a brightness glowed,
    And I, responsive to its strange behest,
Made gentle trespass through the tangled grass
    To where, past ruined plot and tumbled frame,
Crabapple boughs uprose, a leafy mass
    Of reds and saffrons, like a living flame.

Long, long I gazed there, glad that beauty kept
One brave torch burning for a dream that slept.

HOARD

Since I have seen so many summers pass,
    Leaving no tokens but a few late flowers
And prints of silken sandals in the grass,
    I have grown miserly of shining hours.

And I have pilfered from the sprays of June
    Rich souvenirs of sunlight. They are stored
With languors of an August afternoon
    And river-lusters in my secret hoard.

Sylvan transparencies, a flash of wings
    Through orchard boughs, flame in a poppy field,
Brilliants of rain...all these and other things
    Are in my treasury securely sealed.

So when the icy winds assail my eaves
    And not a blade lifts from the frozen mould,
I'll take my treasury of light and leaves
    And gloat again upon the summer's gold.

LIBATION

All garnered is the golden maize,
　　The bins are full, the fruitage stored.
Now toil comes homing through the haze
And now the lessee lifts in praise
　　A chalice to his Overlord.

O not alone for the rich yield
　　And not alone for the fair ranks
Of bundled sheaves upon the field,
And not alone for strength to shield
　　His harvest, glows the steward's thanks.

His grace is said for the benign
　　Unhidden soul in sun and shade,
For unsought God who has His sign
On every star and cloud and vine,
　　For beauty's endless ambuscade.

GRACE AFTER DROUGHT

When from Thy hand a bounteous hoard,
Bright from the reaping, blest my board,
  Did I not thank Thee, Lord?

Now that the harvesting is spare,
Accept for this more frugal fare
  As dutiful a prayer.

For just as nature's ample yield
In other years, from fold and field,
  Thine opulence revealed,

So now these lesser fruits of earth,
Meagerly garnered, by their dearth
  Teach what Thy gifts are worth.

WINTER TOCSIN

Too late, too late, lieutenants of the sun!
　　Foredoomed is all your fiery array.
The summer's forts are falling, one by one,
　　And your last shield will soon be swept away.

Massed goldenrod and bold chrysanthemum,
　　Brave helianthus, doughty marigold,
Against your flanks the northern furies come,
　　And your late lustrous chief is stricken cold.

Call to your colors all the flaming leaves!
　　Recruit the last speared stalk and take your stand.
The foe is ruthless, offers no reprieves,
　　And bears no clemency in his cold hand.

What do the outposts of the asters say?
　　By every road the legions of the frost
Arrive to make your petaled suns their prey
　　And crush you down in one cold holocaust.

"But starlight on the Egypt that shielded Mary's Son!"
(**Ex Ægypto Vocavi Filium Meum**, page 83)

NOW AS LONG AGO

Terce for the Nativity

The Lord hath reigned.
He is clothed with beauty;
The Lord is clothed with strength
And hath girt Himself.
                              —Psalm 92

He Who for our souls' redeeming
Shielded Mary from the scheming
    Perfidies of Lucifer,
Now to make our ransom payment
As a King in fitting raiment
    Takes His royal robe from her.

From that Virgin Tabernacle
Forth He comes to break the shackle
    Gripping us with ancient hurt.
Trembles now the Adversary!
God's own Son, the Son of Mary,
    With the Holy Ghost is girt.

NIGHT OF CONTRADICTION

Judea in the dead of night
    Beholds the morning of our joy,
As Bethlehem by lantern light
    Gives birth to an immortal Boy.

O night of contradicted signs!
    A manger has become a throne;
A star has strayed from its confines
    And stands a sentinel alone.

Far rides a royal caravan
    To this, the least of all the towns;
And there before the Son of Man
    Three wizard Kings take off their crowns.

For this event true patriarch,
    Prophet and seer long have sighed:
Redemption blossoms in the dark
    And Adam's debt is satisfied.

RECESSIONAL

Ah, pilgrim Kings who came to pay
    Your homage to the Light of men,
Was it not hard to turn away
From where the lovely Infant lay
    And take the weary road again?

Swift words were spoken in a dream
    And there was little time to bide.
You had to go, though Heaven's beam
No longer shone; but oh, the gleam
    Of halos on the homeward ride!

Ex Ægypto Vocavi Filium Meum

Egypt, from your silted dream the river-lily nods.
Dust is in your tabernacles. Death is on your gods.
Night is on Ikhnaton, but his spirit in your fanes
Was a witness to the truth, and the truth remains.

Egypt, by your sunken plinths the ibis wades.
Broken lies the obelisk, the hieroglyph fades.
Wilderness of ruin! But a live-forever blooms:
Starry hope deep-hidden in your death-denying tombs.

Egypt, on your templed towns a ten-fold justice fell,
Chastening your tyrant kings, avenging Israel,
But gratitude remembers how you gave a fronded path
To Three in holy hiding from the fang of Herod's wrath.

Egypt of Osiris, let your phantoms sleep.
Egypt of Rameses, may your dream be deep.
To Cleopatra's Egypt a long oblivion;
But starlight on the Egypt that shielded Mary's Son!

Noel in a Time of Peril

Beloved, in this brightest of seasons,
    Forever modern and forever olden,
Let us not yield to terrors or to treasons,
    For faith is fortifying, courage golden.

And let us keep our covenant unbroken
    With those who, when our hearts were half-despairing,
Hurled back with steel the lies that hell had spoken
    And sanctified our freedom with their daring.

"Better the served ideal than the prize!
Better the dared endeavor than the crown!"
(**To One Gallant in Defeat**, page 90)

DREAM ACROSS THE DARK

Dream Across the Dark

Man rives the granite from its ledge
    And wakes the marble from its sleep
Because there is an ancient pledge
    That he is bound to keep.

Some word more subtle than his will,
    Some dream across a dark abyss,
Bids him to make of every hill
    A cold acropolis.

Where cypresses outshade the dark
    With secrets they will never tell,
Agate and alabaster mark
    His hope beyond farewell.

He hears the living plea, and yet
    Upon a stone his tears are shed.
Hearts pulsing warm he may forget,
    But not the silent dead.

THE PALE ROVER

All things at last sweet shelter find
    From sun and frost and fearful stress.
Where life's unmeasured orbits wind
    Only the soul goes shelterless.

Trees to themselves are shield and shade;
    Clouds canopy the naked crags,
And rocky glooms cool the arrayed
    Phalanxes of the waterflags.

The living nerve throbs in its sheath;
    The eye is dusked by silken lids;
Mortality lies proud beneath
    The mosses and the pyramids.

Pale rover in a wilderness,
    By hungers moved, by marvels awed,
Alone the soul walks shelterless
    Under the searching eye of God.

To One Gallant in Defeat

Now let the pulse of aspiration sleep
    A little while, and let the heart have rest.
The trust you undertook and tried to keep
    Lies broken by betrayal and a jest.
Somehow a word went truant at the test
    While ambush lurked upon the hazard steep.
Not yours be the reproach! Not in your breast
    Need the dull bitterness of blame be deep.
Better the served ideal than the prize!
    Better the dared endeavor than the crown!
Better defeat where honor's standard flies
    Than base advantage with that banner down.
So rest. Then rise renewed, and stand restored.
There will be trophies worthy of your sword.

CRYSTAL

The bitterest frost cannot forget
    The ferns its stinging sword has slain,
But by its very breath must set
    Their fronded prints on every pane.

So Death, the icy-fingered one,
    May blight our dreams, but he will see
The windows of oblivion
    Crystaled with immortality.

SONG FOR THE SEEING BLIND

Tricked with the gift of sight,
I stumble through the light,
Bewildered by the gleam
On this earth-anchored dream.
So dazzled are my eyes
By glints of Paradise
Still gold-bright in the grace
Of flower, cloud and face,
My lashes lift afraid
Lest they forget the Maker for the made.

But you whose eyes lie dark
Save for the shielded spark
Of soul-sight, you are led
Unsnared, unwaywarded,
Past every lure, to Him
Whose *fiat lux* could brim
The gulfed abyss of gloom
With incandescent bloom,
Yet in Whose purest sight
Not even Heaven's burnished floor is bright.

FATHER OF LIGHTS

Within this iris-curtained camera
  By which the mind is lensed and given vision,
I held the lamps of universal law
  And marked their steel-bright beauty and precision.
Moon-platinum and Martian phosphor shed
  Balefires therein, backdropped with starry laces,
And I was hyssoped with a holy dread
  That a dim skull could sky the heavenly spaces.
Yet more: In that celled murk the central sun
  Shot the full splendor of his sovereignship's
Superb corona, to my heart's elation.
But most I marveled this: that there is One
  With Whom is neither term nor dark eclipse
Nor shadow-band nor hint of alteration.

LITANY TO LIGHT

Spindrift from the starry rapids,
Foaming sun and flashing comet,
    Fail us not who stand in shadows.

Lash of Leonid and lightning,
Swift flail of the luminous meteor,
    Sting our sight who stand in shadows.

Semaphore across the morning,
Noonday bloom and trellised twilight,
    Give us beauty in the shadows.

Luster of the burnished beetles,
Feather-sheen, wing-iridescence,
    Silken this dull cloth of shadows.

Flicker of the northern streamers,
Ghostly sheeting of the snowdrifts,
    Chill us not who stand in shadows.

Death-script over darkling battle,
Glimmer of forsaken windows,
    Spare us grief who hide in shadows.

Lucifer's lost gift of glory,
Lead us back by glossy traces
    To thy Source, the end of shadows.

THOUGHTS IN A CATHEDRAL

That lover of the light
Who first transfigured broken glass
And blazoned it with sheens and stains
And patterned it in panes
Through which the gleam of God might pass,
His was a more than earthly sleight,
A clear divining and a dare.
From aureoled attendants there,
With sudden flash of inward sight,
He caught the glowing secret which restored
Beauty to worship, peace to prayer
And glory to the temple of the Lord.

And oh, that worker in a dream
Whose forging hand first wrought
The blossom-hinted beauty of a bell!
His was indeed a heavenly theme,
A more than mortal spell.
But who can tell
Whence came that bright symmetric thought
Or what unseen Assistant taught
That hand to shape the metal shell,
To tongue it tunefully and well
And set it swinging, ringing, singing
In praise of Him who watches Israel!

"The hour is come when gentlest voices call
And every lock is wistful for its key ..."
(**Tranquil Hour**, page 98)

TONES AND AFTERTONES

TRANQUIL HOUR

Rich aftertones, chords of tranquillity,
Chime to the weary heart now. Fevers fall.
Taut sinews slacken. Thoughts stir quietly
Like sandaled feet in a Franciscan hall.
The hour is come when gentlest voices call
And every lock is wistful for its key;
The half-light of a legend mantles all,
But insight sharpens and the soul walks free.

Listen! From some awakened instrument
Arpeggios long forgotten pierce the night;
Now memories stir in their sentried camp.
Soft cadences of childhood mirth fall spent,
Rippling the dusk. Doors open to delight
Where love has swept the hearth and trimmed the lamp.

Names

The gods have given every name a tint
    Indelible, a flavor and a fate;
And some are cloudy opals with a glint
    Of stifled flame, and some are plumes of state;
And some are fragrances, and some are flint,
    And some are gloom upon a marble gate.

There's Theodore, a banner; George, a blade;
    And John a constancy when hearts upheave;
And Robert, bugle-blown and unafraid,
    And Harry, laughter; Tony, make-believe;
And Marguerite a star, and Ruth a shade,
    Gay Evelyn and golden Genevieve.

And there's a name that hints of life and death
    And all intensities by these made known;
A name that is as when an organ's breath,
    Suddenly deep, dies in an undertone
While every reed in wonder whispereth:
    That name is his whose love is thine alone.

TOSCANINI BROADCAST

I listened, all sheathed
In lampdusk and stillness,
Till a violin breathed
And there followed a shrillness
Of flutes; soon a cry
Of cornets, then a sullen awaking
Of drums, and my pulses ran high,
And the walls of my spirit were shaking.

Alarum uprose,
All dim to my guessing;
Invisible foes
Were fleeing and pressing.
Whether thunder of wheels
Down the darkness speeding
Or a tumult of heels
Was hid from my heeding.

Hosts fierce, without form,
Met, clashed and divided...
Then the Dantean storm
Receded, subsided;
And I huddled there, hushed
Like a blind man whose face,
Undefended, a fury has brushed,
A terror he cannot trace.

Discipline

A reveler at heart, he stirred
  To every gust of golden din,
But in a secret ear he heard
  The warning drums of discipline.

"Seek," Pleasure said, "this lilied rest;
  There is no whiter goal to win."
But to his laggard will he pressed
  The tempered spur of discipline.

Men asked him in the castle yard
  By what door he had entered in.
His answer was: "No sentry barred
  The iron door of discipline."

COBWEBS

When the human hustle ebbs
From a once hive-busy place,
Mildew, dust and spider webs
Move right in with quiet pace,
Turning lint to musty lace,
Etching woodwork, tool and desk
With an artless arabesque.

Neither idleness nor death
Wins a vantage in that air;
Industries of gentler breath
Skip across the stillness there.
Every corner, niche and room
Holds a hint of silk and loom.
Forms of life, with soundless hum,
Fill the unfeared vacuum.

Clifford J. Laube

LONG AFTER RAIN

Long after rain has swept the summer grove,
    Drenching the fern-embroidered forest strip,
The woodsman hears, deep in his shadow-cove,
    A ghostlier rain, the eerie under-drip.

Long after anger in the shaken heart
    Is quelled and canceled, claiming no arrears,
There still remains, half solace and half smart,
    The eloquence of unconfided tears.

MOMENT ON ABENAKI

Where birch and balsam sought embrace
    And mosses made a restful stair,
In stillness by your passive grace
    I held you close and kissed your hair.

As wild and free was that caress
    As the white clouds that raced above.
I loved you for your loveliness;
    Surely you loved me for my love.

Clifford J. Laube

SENTRIES

Midnight. The maples stir. The stars are lost.
  A cold mist rises from the Rockaways.
September trembles with a fear of frost;
  Darkness ingathers all the ghosts of days.

The stars are lost. The midnight web is spun.
  Sad autumn to her somber breast receives
What summertime forsakes. I think of one
  Who walked with me through silences of leaves.

O midnight maples, once this heart could feed
  On misty shadows with a strange delight;
But now it hungers to a holier need.
  Forgive me, sentries of the starless night!

"You are my faith amid the unfulfilled;
You are my relay to a farther goal."
(**To My Son**, page 110)

THE POWER AND THE GLORY

To a Child Asleep

Light-hearted sleeper
    Folded in fleece,
Your rest is deeper
    Than a cloud's peace.

My heart is billowed
    On a wild upswell,
Seeing you pillowed
    In night's vast spell.

Your quiet breathing
    Makes me glad
Of an old heart-seething
    And a dream I've had.

THE ARCHER

I once had a daughter,
    A spirited child,
Merry as mountain water,
    And as wild.

She was the creature
    My dream had designed,
Elfin of form and feature,
    Elfin of mind.

Hour on hour
    She danced in my sight,
Gay as a bird or flower
    In sunlight.

"Oh, I'd never bother
    To love anyone
As much as my father!"
    Was the song she spun.

But my heart, foreknowing,
    Was troubled and sad
At the wild glowing
    Way she had.

Not long thereafter
    An archer came by
With arrows of laughter,
    And aim in his eye.

Soon, as his winging
    Shadow crossed her,
She ceased her singing.
    I had lost her.

To My Son

What have I to give you, my fond-eyed boy?
    Or what indeed have I the power to give
In fair return for this unshadowed joy—
    This bond whereby in you I doubly live?

You are my faith amid the unfulfilled;
    You are my relay to a farther goal.
You are a voice to throb when mine is stilled;
    You are another garment for my soul.

I have but given for your venturing
    A heart's white heat, vibration and a breath,
But you have given me a dare to fling
    Across the echoless dark wall of death.

Clifford J. Laube

To Christopher, My Grandson

That ferryman, that saint
Whose ancient Lycian fame
Still flowers in your name,
For all his strength grew faint
Bearing his Infant Lord
Across the swollen ford,
And sensing in that freight
Our ransom's fearful weight.

But gentle grandson, you,
A child of scarcely two
Here in my circling arm,
By some intrinsic art
Of innocence and charm,
Have lifted from my heart
Weights that had worn me down,
Late trudging toward that Town
Of termless Light descried
Beyond this riverside.

*"To her with twelve grouped in an upper room
It came in swirls of Pentecostal bloom..."*
(**As Shadow and As Flame**, page 116)

SIGNATURE AND COUNTERSIGN

COUNTERSIGN

O brown deep-bodied earth, since that first morning
    When with awareness waking to delight
I saw you garlanded in glad adorning
    From lilied valley to the laureled height,
    Yet naked to my need by day or night,

I have kept fresh that dream, that early wonder
    So like a seal upon my spirit pressed,
Making your lights my play, your fruits my plunder,
    Your sounds my silence and your rocks my rest.

Whatever wing or snowflake caught my fancy,
    Whatever whisper by a windy shore,
Whatever sleight of your rich geomancy,
    Agate or rose-quartz from your crystal core,
    Freely you made it mine, and offered more.

Now in this heartlift be not less rewarded.
    Here is my signature, my countersign.
That early dream remains. It shall be guarded.
    Your gladness, under God, has armored mine.

BIDDEN WORD

Traveling down the metered years,
    I have had friends, a cherished few,
Who were to me through joy and tears
    A royal-hearted retinue.

And some were old, some in their prime,
    And some were lads still morning-eyed,
Comrades in revelry and rhyme;
    And some are fled, and some have died.

In their confiding company,
    Having no secret word to keep,
I could speak candidly and free;
    Could sift things delicate and deep.

With them I never thought it shame
    To talk of rivers, stars and ferns;
Of music, shadows, altar-flame
    And faith and all that faith discerns.

For those remembered ones and dear
    There is a bidden word to say:
I walked in light when they were near,
    In twilight when they went away.

As Shadow and as Flame

New Gospel insights gleam like ores refined
When Blessed Mary looms in heart and mind.

How fittingly the Holy Spirit came
To her—as shadow first, and then as flame!

Shaded It came to her in Galilee
As suited her chaste humility;

But later, she wore her sorrow-crown,
So like her Son's, in stricken Shalom-town,

To her with twelve grouped in an upper room
It came in swirls of Pentecostal bloom,

Thus sealing for all time her central role
As Mother of Christ's Church—its heart, its soul.

RENEWAL

When I was twelve years old I vowed
By rill and rock, by star and cloud,
I would be joyous, free and proud.

All that I knew and all I cared
Was that a Power had prepared
A world of gifts in which I shared.

Now at my life's meridian
I stand, as on a hill, and scan,
Still glad, the beauty of His plan.

By night and day, in every place,
I feel a consecrating grace
Still cool as then upon my face.

Even as then I find no shame
In body, senses, soul and flame,
Knowing from whose white Hand they came.

All that I know and all I care
Is what I learned with my first prayer:
That God is here and everywhere.

And so that light I swear to keep
Till I have stumbled down the steep
To my last hope-illumined sleep.

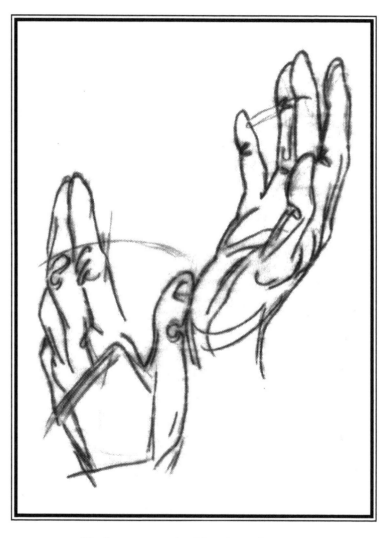

"So from your weaving I have learned to weave
Some wisps of borrowed splendor in your sight..."
(**Sunset Song to the Spinner of Life,** page 120)

EPILOGUE

Sunset Song to the Spinner of Life

Power supreme, O Spirit infinite
Maker of atom, molecule and cell,
Sourcelight from whom all other lights are lit,
Master who teaches wisdom how to spell,
Love how to bloom and courage how to climb,
I marvel that your love has wrought for me
This lustrous scarf of life, this cloth of time,
Out of the tissues of eternity.

Inscrutable, O Weaver, are the looms
Where amid music of mysterious reels
And whirring spindles you have fashioned forth
This silk not made for tear-stains nor for tombs,
This living textile, glossed with rosy seals,
One more brave banner linking heaven and earth.

As an apprentice, striving to achieve
Pure mastery, marks well his tutor's skill
And weds its disciplines to his own will,
So from your weaving I have learned to weave
Some wisps of borrowed splendor in your sight,
Pale mirror-gleams of your primordial light.

Lord, if this life-stuff that I wear and am,
This garment bearing your bright monogram,
Had by some hid design been dealt to me
In meager dole-lengths down through shortened days,
Still would the pattern prove your artistry,
Still would the damask shimmer with your praise.

Yet, Master-spinner, wondrously your will
Has processed more than richly for my sake,
Through threescore years and ten, unstinted skeins
Of life and strength in love's glad give and take,
Till now at last, still threadfast to its mill,
The weight-enwearied fabric thins and strains.

Lord, you have heard my lauds, my chansonnettes.
Hear my entreaty now: Let not this stole
Of selfhood slip from the strong spinnerets
That fashioned it, unfurled it, flesh and soul.
Cast it not from your grand economy
Like some cold shred of orbital debris.

But let its silk, though frayed, be repossessed.
Spool it back, Sire, to your spinning rooms,
Unravel it and let its fibers rest;
Restore its stitchwork, freed of seams and scars,
Then flash it forth anew from your vast looms,
A flag of witness in the wash of stars.

CPSIA information can be obtained
at www.ICGtesting.com
Printed in the USA
FSHW020802030419
56871FS